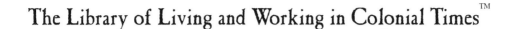

# A Day in the Life of a Colonial Surveyor

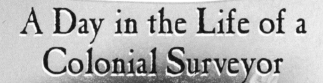

Amy French Merrill

The Rosen Publishing Group's
PowerKids Press™
New York

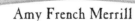

*For Sunita*

Published in 2002 by The Rosen Publishing Group, Inc.
29 East 21st Street, New York, NY 10010

First Edition

Book Design: Danielle Primiceri
Layout Design: Maria E. Melendez and Nick Sciacca
Project Editor: Frances E. Ruffin

Photo Credits: Title page, pp. 4, 7, 8, 12, 15, 16, 20 © North Wind Picture Archives; pp. 11, 19 © The Granger Collection, New York.

Merrill, Amy French.
A day in the life of a colonial surveyor / Amy French Merrill.
    p. cm. — (The Library of living and working in colonial times)
ISBN 0-8239-5823-X
1.  Surveying—United States—History—18th century—Juvenile literature. 2.  Surveyors—United States—History—18th century—Juvenile literature. [1. Surveying—History—18th century. 2. United States—History—Colonial period, ca. 1600–1775.] I. Title. II. Series.
TA521 .B74 2002
526.9'0974'09034—dc21

2001000252

Manufactured in the United States of America

# Contents

# Looking for Adventure

During the summer of 1731, Jared Johnson was on a month-long trip through the **colony** of Maryland. Jared was a surveyor. Surveyors explored areas of land by measuring and recording the locations of forests, fields, rivers, and mountains. Jared's family lived on a small farm in eastern Maryland. He liked the farm, but when a surveyor named Paul Thomas advertised for an assistant, Jared applied for the job. He was to accompany Paul's team of surveyors on a trip across Maryland. At the age of 16, Jared became a surveyor.

*Surveyors often camped outdoors. In this drawing, surveyors are shown laying out what would become the city of Baltimore.*

# Land in the New World

In a new world full of unexplored land, surveyors had a very important job. Paul Thomas and his men had been hired by one of Maryland's county surveyors. A county surveyor was in charge of land **grants**. Before a person was given a grant for ownership of a piece of land, surveyors decided on the **boundaries** of each piece. Jared would help Paul and his team of surveyors to study the land near the border that separated the colony of Maryland from the colony of Virginia.

*This is a map of Maryland and Virginia. The two colonies had many disagreements about the border that separated them.* ▶

MARYLAND

VIRGINIA

VIRGINIA. 1738.

# Becoming a Surveyor

As Jared helped Paul to saddle up their horses, he thought about how fortunate he was. Surveying was one of the most important **trades** in colonial America. Some surveyors had taught themselves. Paul Thomas had learned most of his skills from reading books and watching other surveyors. Jared also had studied surveying books, and even had practiced doing small surveys on his family's farm. Paul Thomas believed that the best way to learn was through experience. Jared had to agree. He had learned so much already!

◀ *This painting shows a team of early American surveyors.*

# Traveling in the Colonies

After eating a quick breakfast of smoked meat and dried berries, Paul Thomas and Jared set off on foot through the woods. The other men on their team rode the horses. When the men on horseback had traveled a certain distance, they stopped, tied the horses, and continued on foot. When Jared and Paul came upon the horses, they took their turn to ride. In this way, the four men shared two horses. This system was called ride-and-tie. Jared carried his surveying tools on his back, along with his sleeping blankets and food.

*The English team of Charles Mason and Jeremiah Dixon (shown right) surveyed a boundary between Pennsylvania and Maryland known as the Mason-Dixon Line.* ▶

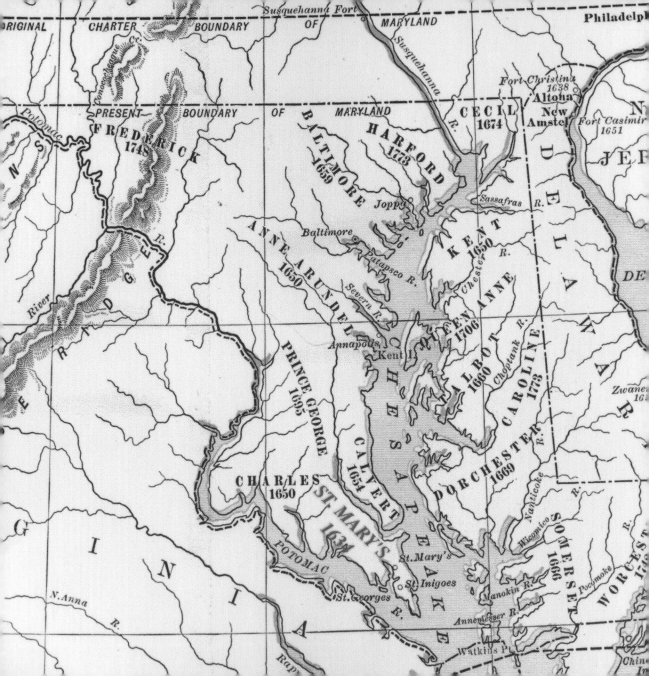

# Unseen Places

Jared had started his trip at the mouth of the Potomac River, right near St. Mary's City, Maryland's first town. This was a **port** town. Jared was amazed to see all of the boats that had been at sea for months. They had carried goods all the way from Europe to be sold in American colonies. From St. Mary's City, the surveying team traveled to western Maryland, where there were few towns. They traveled past farms, which had hundreds of **acres** (hectares) of land. Soon Jared saw nothing but forests for miles around.

◄ *This map of Maryland locates St. Mary's City. The colony was growing rapidly. A new city, Baltimore, was founded in 1729.*

# Surveying Instruments

Surveyors used many different instruments. Jared was familiar with the shiny brass **compass**. Surveyors also used a jacob staff. This was a long, wooden rod that was pushed firmly into the ground to hold their instruments steady. Jared set his compass on the other end. One of the most important surveying tools was the set of chain and stakes that was used to measure distance. The chain had 100 links, and it measured a total of 66 feet (20 m). Paul directed Jared to move the long chain from one location to another.

*This woodcut of a surveyor's instruments shows a jacob staff with a compass and other instruments mounted on it.* ▶

# Measuring Land

After traveling for several hours, Paul signaled to stop. He instructed Jared to set up the chain with a stake at one of the chain's ends. To count out a long distance, Jared placed a stake at one end of the chain, then he moved the chain and put a stake at the other end. To measure 1 acre (.4 ha) of land, Jared had to measure a square that was about the length of ten chains on each side. As they worked, Paul and the other surveyors gave Jared directions, often using words that only surveyors understood.

◀ *George Washington was a surveyor before he commanded the Continental army and became the first U.S. president in 1789.*

# Mapping the Land

Jared and the other surveyors wrote down measurements all afternoon. They described the locations of streams, hills, and different types of trees. Surveyors also made maps of the land they surveyed. Many colonial maps were drawn with pen and ink and painted with watercolors. They were real works of art. Surveyors also drew contour maps. A contour map showed the elevation, or height of the land, at different levels. Making an accurate map of any kind took skill and practice.

*Events like hurricanes could reshape a coastline so new maps were always needed. This 1718 map shows the Mississippi Valley and the Gulf of Mexico. There are many hurricanes in the Gulf of Mexico.*

# A Man of Many Talents

Many colonial surveyors were well-educated men. One of the greatest surveyors of the 18th century was a man named Benjamin Banneker. He lived at a time when most black people in America were slaves. They were not permitted to learn to read or to write. Benjamin was an African American who was born free. He was a farmer who studied to become a surveyor, inventor, **engineer**, **mathematician**, **astronomer**, and an author. Benjamin Banneker was one of the surveyors who planned the city of Washington, D.C.

◀ *This is a portrait of Benjamin Banneker, a man of great achievements.*

# Sleeping Under the Stars

At the end of a long day, Jared was glad to rest. He helped to gather wood and build a fire. Paul Thomas slowly roasted a **passenger pigeon**. The men usually ate dried meat, fish, fruits, and berries. Sometimes they caught fresh fish or hunted birds to eat. After eating, the men played cards around the fire. As the sky grew dark, Paul pointed out the **constellations** in the night sky. Jared listened to stories of the men's travels surveying new lands. Closing his eyes, Jared knew that someday he would have stories of his own to tell.

# Glossary

**acres** (AY-kerz)  Units of area used to measure land.

**astronomer** (uh-STRAH-nuh-mer)  A scientist who studies the Sun, Moon, planets, and stars.

**boundaries** (BOWN-duh-reez)  Another word for borders.

**colony** (KAH-luh-nee)  An area in a new country which is still ruled by the leaders and laws of the old country.

**compass** (KUM-pass)  A tool used to determine the direction of north, south, east, and west.

**constellations** (kahn-stuh-LAY-shunz)  A group of stars that, when viewed together, appear to form a figure or design.

**engineer** (en-jih-NEER)  A person who is an expert at planning and building engines, machines, roads, bridges, and canals.

**grants** (GRANTS)  Legal documents that entitle their holders to a set piece of land.

**mathematician** (math-muh-TIH-shun)  One who studies arithmetic and the science of numbers, measurements, and shapes.

**passenger pigeon** (PAS-in-jer PIH-jin)  An extinct bird that was plentiful in eastern North America.

**port** (PORT)  A city or town on a large body of water where ships come to dock and trade.

**trades** (TRAYDZ)  Any work done with the hands that requires special training.

# Index

# Web Sites

For more information about colonial surveyors, check out these Web sites:

http://rs6.loc.gov/ammem/gmdhtml/gwmaps.html

www.princeton.edu/~mcbrown/display/banneker.html#T